The Story of a Special Day
Volume 75

March 15

74th day of the year
(75th in leap years)
291 days remaining
until the end of the year.

by Michael Dobson

Timespinner
Press

For more information about the series, about me, or
about your special day, please email us at
editor@timespinnerpress.com.

Look for other volumes in *The Story of a Special Day*,
coming often.

Table of Contents

Cover: *La Morte di Cesare (The Death of Caesar)*, by Vincenzo Camuccini, for the Event of the Day.

Back Cover: The month of March, from the French Gothic illuminated manuscript *Les Très Riches Heures du duc de Berry.*

March 15 Quotations

"You know more than you think you do."

— Dr. Benjamin Spock, died March 15, 1998

"I consider a good reputation is a great part of the human happiness. Some people, if they are very, very rich can permit themselves certain negligence to their reputations."

— Aristotle Onassis, died March 15, 1975

"History moves in contradictions. The skeleton of historic existence, the economic structure of society, also develops in contradictions. Forms eternally follow forms. Everything has only a passing being. The dynamic force of life creates the new over and over again — such is the law inherent in reality."

— Nikolai Bukharin, died March 15, 1938

"Dissents speak to a future age. It's not simply to say, 'My colleagues are wrong and I would do it this way.' But the greatest dissents do become court opinions and gradually over time their views become the dominant view. So that's the dissenter's hope: that they are writing not for today but for tomorrow."

— *Justice Ruth Bader Ginsburg,*
born March 15, 1933

"It is a damn poor mind indeed which can't think of at least two ways to spell any word."

— *Andrew Jackson, born March 15, 1767*

"I'd rather betray others, than have others betray me."

— *Emperor Cao Cao, died March 15, 220 CE*

"Men willingly believe what they wish."

— *Julius Caesar, died March 15, 44 BCE*

Event of the Day

The Assassination of Julius Caesar

"Beware the Ides of March!" says the soothsayer to Julius Caesar in Shakespeare's play, but the warning failed to take. On March 15, 44 BCE, a group of 60 members of the Roman Senate, led by Marcus Junius Brutus and Gaius Cassius Longinus — better known to history as Brutus and Cassius — ambushed Caesar and stabbed him 23 times.

Born into an aristocratic family, Gaius Julius Caesar had been intimately involved in the intrigues and bloodshed that marked the last century of the Roman Republic. Torn by a bitter rivalry between the traditionalist Optimates and the reformist Populares, Rome several times descended into civil war. In that environment, the young Caesar won a major military award, the Civic Crown (a crown of oak leaves, often seen in portraits of Caesar), survived kidnapping by pirates, served in the war against Spartacus, administered Spain, and was elected Pontifex Maximum, chief priest of the Roman religion.

As a member of the Populares, Caesar made bitter enemies among the Optimates, and survived only through making an alliance with Pompey the Great and Crassus, known to history as the First Triumvirate. Caesar was elected consul in 59 BCE, and following his consulship, arranged to gain command in southern France, from which he launched his conquest of Gaul.

His enemies continued to intrigue against him. His ally in the First Triumvirate, Crassus, died on a military campaign in the east, and his other partner, Pompey the Great (married to Caesar's daughter), changed sides after the death of his wife, because of his growing jealousy of Caesar's accomplishments. The Optimates arranged to have Caesar stripped of power, but instead Caesar crossed the Rubicon River and civil war broke out.

Caesar was triumphant in the Civil War, defeating Pompey and his long-time enemy Cato — although he took some time off to romance the Egyptian queen Cleopatra. Returning to Rome, Caesar was appointed Dictator, a traditional office, with the goal of reforming the dysfunctional Roman government. He carried out land reforms, calendar reforms, built public works, and made constitutional changes. He extended his dictatorship several times, eventually being named Dictator in Perpetuity.

His next goal was to conquer the Parthian Empire, whose forces had killed his old partner Crassus. As he prepared to leave on his next military campaign, a group of conspirators known as the Liberatores began to plot an end to Caesar's rule. Luring Caesar to Pompey's Theater, the conspirators surrounded Caesar. A man named Casca struck first. As Caesar struggled to get away, eyes blinded by blood, the assassins continued to stab him until he died.

There is no evidence that Caesar actually said, "Et tu, Brute?" It was, however, a particularly important betrayal. Brutus's mother had been Caesar's mistress, and some have suggested that Brutus was actually Caesar's son — though Caesar would only have been 15 at the time.

Although the Liberatores expected that they would be honored and that traditional Rome would be restored, they would be bitterly disappointed. Caesar's death led to the final civil war of the Roman Republic. After 13 years of war, Caesar's nephew and heir Octavian ended up sole ruler of Rome, and is thus considered the first emperor of the Roman Empire.

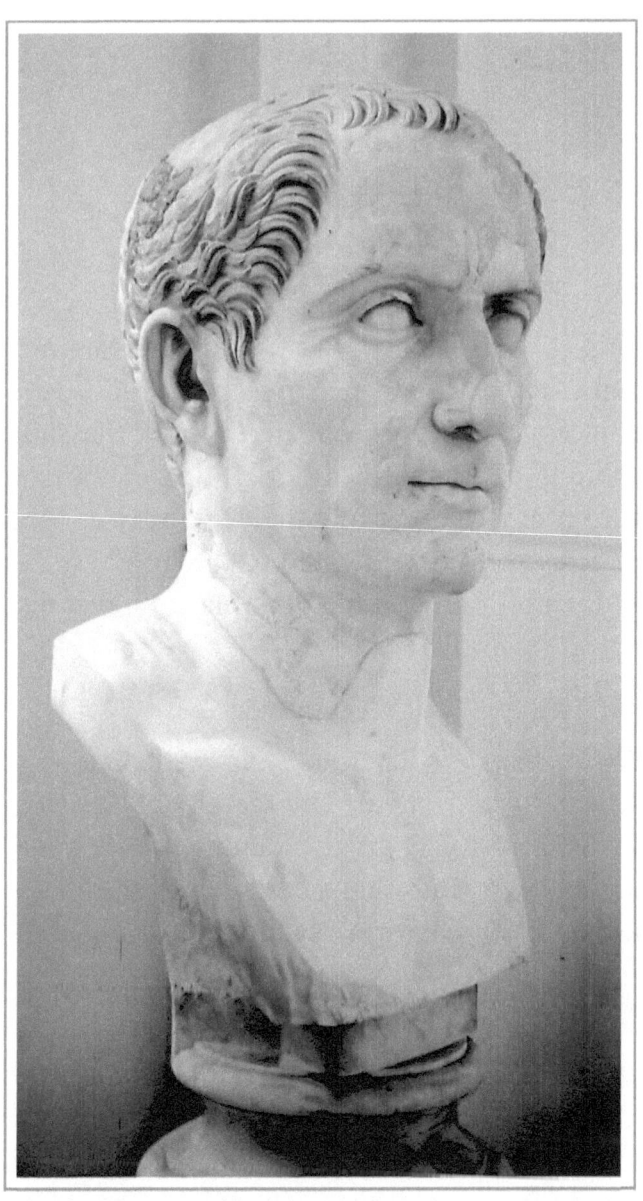

Bust of Julius Caesar

March 15 Holidays and Celebrations

Ides of March (Roman Empire)

Each month in the Roman calendar has three special days: Kalends, the first day of the month (origin of "calendar"), Nones, the ninth day of the month, and Ides, the middle of the month (15th day of March, May, July, and October and the 13th day of other months). The Ides of March was a festive day dedicated to the god Mars, and usually a military parade took place on that day.

Hōnen Matsuri (豊年祭) (Japan)

Hōnen means "prosperous year" in Japanese, and a *matsuri* is a festival. On March 15, the Hōnen Matsuri fertility festival includes parades and is marked by phallus-shaped souvenirs and in some places all-you-can drink sake.

National Day (Hungary)

National Day in Hungary, celebrated on March 15, is the memorial day of the 1848 Revolution against the Austrian Empire. People wear cockade hats with the national colors of red, white, and green.

Rise Up, Hungarian! by János Thorma

Constitution Day (Дзень Канстытуцыі) (Belarus)

The Republic of Belarus approved its post-Soviet constitution on March 15, 1994, and they celebrate Constitution Day each March 15.

Christian Feast Days

Saints commemorated on March 15 include Clemens Maria Hofbauer, Leocritia, Louise de Marillac, and Raymond of Fitero.

What Happened on March 15?

The abbreviation "O.S." on some dates refers to the fact that the Russian Empire did not switch from the Julian to the Gregorian calendar at the same time as the rest of Europe, and therefore some figures have two dates for their birth or death.

People whose original names are not in the Western alphabet have their native names in the appropriate script shown in parenthesis.

1493 CE - Columbus Returns to Spain

On March 15, 1493, Christopher Columbus returned from his first voyage to the New World, landing in Barcelona to a hero's reception. For the first time, Europe saw tobacco, pineapple, a turkey, and the hammock, originally developed in Central and South America.

1672 CE - Charles II issues the Royal Declaration of Indulgence

Following the establishment of the independent Church of England by Henry VIII, Catholics, along with Protestant nonconformists, suffered increasingly harsh penalties for their religion. On March 15, 1672, King Charles II suspendent those "penal laws" in the Royal Declaration of Indulgence. The Parliament overruled him, however, and implemented new laws forbidding Catholic officeholders. When Charles II's Catholic son James II tried to issue a similar declaration, it led to the Glorious Revolution that ousted James II from the throne.

Charles II of England by Peter Lely

1781 CE - Battle of Guilford Courthouse

The Battle of Guilford Courthouse, which took place on March 15, 1781, in Greensboro, North Carolina, ended in American defeat when British soldiers commanded by General Charles Cornwallis defeated a much larger force of Americans. Instead of pursuing his victory, Cornwallis turned north to meet up with Benedict Arnold, but ended up losing to George Washington at Yorktown, ending the war.

Battle of Guilford Court House

1783 CE - Washington Ends the Newburgh Conspiracy

The Newburgh Conspiracy was a near-rebellion of the Continental Army after the Revolutionary War out of fear that the new country's Congress wouldn't provide back pay and pensions as they had promised. On March 5, 1783, George Washington called a meeting of the leaders and gave a speech that "moved to tears" many of the assembled officers, who re-pledged their loyalty to the United States. Congress eventually paid part of what they had promised, but in the meantime, financier Robert Morris spent over $800,000 of his own money to pay the soldiers, the equivalent of well over $20 million today.

1820 CE - Maine Becomes a State

In 1820, Maine, which had been part of Massachusetts, seceded to form its own state, and was admitted to the Union on March 15.

1848 CE - Hungarian Revolution

Beginning on March 15, 1848, peaceful mass demonstrations in Buda and Pest forced the Hungarian government to agree to a list of demands for democratic reform. Hungarian National Day celebrates this event.

1906 CE - Rolls-Royce is Founded

On March 15, 1906, car dealer Charles Stewart Rolls and car builder Sir Frederick Henry Royce turned their partnership into a new corporation, Rolls-Royce, Ltd., which made iconic high-quality cars. The car business, now consisting of Rolls-Royce and Bentley, was sold to Volkswagen and the Rolls-Royce name was licensed to BMW. The two companies compromised, and now BMW makes Rolls-Royce and Volkswagen makes Bentley.

1905 Rolls-Royce 10HP

1917 CE - The Last Tsar Abdicates

Nicholas II (Николай II), Tsar of Russia, abdicated the throne on March 15 [O.S. March 2], 1917. He and his family were imprisoned, and later were killed by the Bolsheviks.

Russian Royal Family, 1913 (l to r): Olga, Maria, Nicholas II, Alexandra Fyodorovna, Anastasia, Alexei, and Tatiana

1956 CE - *My Fair Lady* Broadway Premiere

The stage musical *My Fair Lady*, based on George Bernard Shaw's *Pygmalion*, premiered on Broadway on this day in 1956. It ran for a record 2,717 performances and spawned the best-selling album in the U.S. in 1956.

1985 CE - First Domain Name

On March 15, 1985, the computer manufacturer Symbolics, Inc., registered the first dot-com domain in the world: symbolics.com. The company was sold in 2009.

1990 CE - "Two Plus Four Agreement" Reunites Germany

The Potsdam Agreement of 1945 resulted in two Germanies: Soviet-aligned East Germany and Western-aligned West Germany. On March 15, 1991, the "Treaty on the Final Settlement With Respect to Germany" formally ended the occupation of Germany and opened the door to a reunited Germany.

2011 CE - Syrian Civil War

On March 15, 2011, the Arab Spring reached Syria, with massive demonstrations and protests nationwide against the ruling Ba'ath government under President Bashar al-Assad (بشار حافظ الأسد). In April, the Syrian Army was sent to stop the uprising, and civil war broke out.

Who Was Born
on March 15?

Acting and Film

Adrianne León (March 15, 1987 —)

León won a daytime enemy as the punk rock teen Brook in *General Hospital*, played Colleen Carlton in *The Young and the Restless*, and is the lead vocalist of the rock band Caught Crimson.

Kellan Lutz (March 15, 1985 —)

Lutz is known for playing Emmett Cullen in the *Twilight Saga* films.

Sean Biggerstaff (March 15, 1983 —)

Scottish actor Biggerstaff played quiddich captain Oliver Wood in the *Harry Potter* films.

Eva Longoria (March 15, 1975 —)

Longoria played Isabella on *The Young and the Restless* and Gabrielle on *Desperate Housewives*.

Kim Raver (March 15, 1969 —)

Raver was Kim on *Third Watch*, Audrey on *24*, and Teddy on *Grey's Anatomy*.

Jimmy Baio (March 15, 1962 —)

Jimmy Baio, a cousin of actor Scott Baio, is best known for playing Billy Tate in the TV sitcom *Soap*.

Renny Harlin (March 15, 1959 —)

Finnish-American film director Lauri Mauritz Harjola, better known as Renny Harlin, directed *Die Hard 2, Cliffhanger,* and numerous other films. He is married to actress Geena Davis.

David Silverman (March 15, 1957 —)

Animator David Silverman directed *The Simpsons Movie* as well as numerous episodes of the TV series, and created most of the "rules" for drawing the Simpsons.

Joaquim de Almeida (March 15, 1957 —)

De Almeida (right) played the villain in 1994's *Clear and Present Danger* and a season of the TV series *24*. He has also had major roles in numerous international film and stage productions.

Craig Wasson (March 15, 1954 —)

Wasson starred in the 1984 Brian DePalma film *Body Double* and played Doug Ebert in the soap opera *One Life to Live*.

David Cronenberg (March 15, 1943 —)

Filmmaker David Cronenberg is best known for his work in the "body horror" genre. His films include *Videodrome,* the 1986 remake of *The Fly*, *Rabid*, and *Crash.*

Judd Hirsch (March 15, 1935 —)

Hirsch is known for his starring roles in the TV series *Taxi* and *Numb3rs*, and received an Academy Award nomination for his work in 1980's *Ordinary People.*

Philippe de Broca (March 15, 1933 — November 26, 2004)

French film director de Broca is known for his films *Cartouche* and *L'Homme de Rio*. He received the Legion of Honor for contributions to French culture.

Christian Marquand (March 15, 1927 — November 22, 2000)

Marquand was in 1956's *Et Dieu créa la femme (And God Created Woman)* with Brigitte Bardot, and appeared in numerous American films including *The Longest Day, Lord Jim,* and *Flight of the Phoenix*. He also directed the 1968 film *Candy*.

Walter Gotell (March 15, 1924 — May 5, 1997)

German-British actor Gotell played the head of the KGB in six James Bond films.

Lawrence Tierney (March 15, 1919 — February 26, 2002)

Tierney usually played mobsters and criminals, including the title role in 1945's *Dillinger*.

Frank Coghlan, Jr. (March 15, 1916 — September 7, 2009)

Child actor Coghlan is known for playing Billy Batson in the serial *Adventures of Captain Marvel.* He went on to a 23 year career as a naval aviator.

Joe E. Ross (March 15, 1914 — August 13, 1982)

Ross starred in sitcoms including *The Phil Silvers Show* and *Car 54, Where Are You?*

(left, with co-star Fred Gwynne) He is known for his trademark exclamation "Ooh! Ooh!"

Macdonald Carey (March 15, 1913 — March 21, 1994)

Carey played Dr. Tom Horton on *Days of Our Lives* for nearly 30 years.

Nick Stewart (March 15, 1910 — December 18, 2000)

Stewart played Lightnin' on the *Amos and Andy* television series.

George Brent (March 15, 1889 — May 26, 1979)

Bette Davis's most frequent co-star, Brent starred opposite Davis in 13 films including *Jezebel* and *Dark Victory*. Prior to his film career, he was part of an IRA Active Service Unit and left Ireland with a British bounty on his head.

Art

Naoko Takeuchi (武内 直子) (March 15, 1967 —)

Japanese manga artist Naoko Takeuchi created *Sailor Moon*.

Business

Marjorie Merriweather Post (March 15, 1887 — September 12, 1973)

Daughter of cereal magnate C. W. Post, Marjorie founded General Foods, Inc., becoming the wealthiest woman in America. Her $250 million fortune is the equivalent of over $5 billion today.

Crime

Aniello Dellacroce (March 15, 1914 — December 2, 1985)

Dellacroce, known as "the Tall Guy," was underboss of the Gambino crime family.

Music

Honey Singh (March 15, 1984 —)

Punjabi rapper and singer Honey Singh produces music for Bollywood films and is currently the highest-paid Indian musical artist.

will.i.am (March 15, 1975 —)

William J. Adams, better known by his stage name, was a founder of The Black Eyed Peas, and has won seven Grammys, eight American Music Awards, and three World Music Awards.

Fergie and will.i.am (right)

Terence Trent D'Arby (March 15, 1962 —)

Under his stage name Terence Trent D'Arby, Terence Howard sold over 14 million copies of his debut album *Introducing the Hardline According to Terence Trent D'Arby*. Following a series of dreams in 1995, he legally changed his name to Sananda Maitreya and continues to record.

Ry Cooder (March 15, 1947 —)

Cooder is ranked 8th on *Rolling Stone* magazine's 2003 list of the 100 greatest guitarists of all time.

Sly Stone (March 15, 1943 —)

Under his stage name, Sylvester Stewart is best known as the frontman for Sly and the Family Stone. He was inducted into the Rock and Roll Hall of Fame in 1993.

Mike Love (March 15, 1941 —)

Mike Love was a founding member of The Beach Boys, and with the group is a member of the Rock and Roll Hall of Fame. He wrote lyrics for "Surfin' Safari," "I Get Around," and "Good Vibrations."

Phil Lesh (March 15, 1940 —)

Bass guitarist Phil Lesh was a founding member of the Grateful Dead.

Howard Greenfield (March 15, 1936 — March 4, 1986)

Brill Building mainstay Howard Greenfield wrote lyrics for such hits as "Breaking Up Is Hard To Do," "Everybody's Somebody's Fool," "Love Will Keep Us Together," and "Venus in Blue Jeans." He also co-wrote theme songs for the TV shows *Bewitched* and *The Flying Nun*.

D. J. Fontana (March 15, 1931 —)

Fontana was the drummer for Elvis Presley, playing on over 460 RCA cuts with Elvis.

Carl Smith (March 15, 1927 — January 16, 2010)

Known as "Mister Country," Smith was one of the most successful male artists in the genre in the 1950s, with thirty Top 10 hits. He was married to June Carter, who subsequently became June Carter Cash. Smith is a member of the Country Music Hall of Fame.

Harry James (March 15, 1916 — July 5, 1983)

Trumpeter and swing band leader Harry James was the first well-known bandleader to employ Frank Sinatra.

Lightnin' Hopkins (March 15, 1912 — January 30, 1983)

Country blues singer and guitarist Sam John Hopkins is on *Rolling Stone's* list of the greatest 100 guitarists of all time.

Lightnin' Hopkins, painted by Jules Grandgagnage

Eduard Strauss (March 15, 1835 — December 28, 1916)

Austrian waltz and polka composer Eduard Strauss was the brother of "Waltz King" Johann Strauss and part of the Strauss musical dynasty that included his father and another brother.

Newsmakers

Takeru Kobayashi (小林尊) (March 15, 1978 —)

Japanese competitive eater Kobayashi holds four Guinness Records for eating hot dogs, meatballs, Twinkies, hamburgers, and pasta.

Penny Lancaster (March 15, 1971 —)

Lingerie model Penny Lancaster is married to rock singer Rod Stewart.

Politics and Law

Ruth Bader Ginsburg (March 15, 1933 —)

Ginsburg (right) was the second female justice of the U.S. Supreme Court.

Richard Wirthlin (March 15, 1931 — March 16, 2011)

Pollster Richard Wirthlin was best known as Ronald Reagan's chief strategist.

Berthold Schenk Graf von Stauffenberg (March 15, 1905 — August 10, 1944)

Brother of would-be Hitler assassin Claus von Stauffenberg, Berthold was part of the July 20, 1944 plot against Hitler, and was subsequently executed by the Nazi regime.

Harold L. Ickes (March 15, 1874 — February 3, 1952)

Ickes served as Secretary of the Interior under FDR for a record-setting 13 years, and was responsible for implementing much of the "New Deal."

John Henry Kagi (March 15, 1835 — October 17, 1859)

Attorney and abolitionist Kagi was second-in-command in John Brown's raid on Harper's Ferry, and was killed in that battle.

Andrew Jackson (March 15, 1767 — June 8, 1845)

Andrew Jackson, nicknamed "Old Hickory," was the seventh President of the United States. His followers created the modern Democratic Party.

Andrew Jackson

Religion

Jimmy Swaggart (March 15, 1935 —)

Pentecostal televangelist Jimmy Swaggart was involved in a sex scandal in the late 1980s. He is a cousin of rockabilly pioneer Jerry Lee Lewis and country star Mickey Gilley.

Science and Space

Alan Bean (March 15, 1932 —)

Astronaut Alan Bean became the fourth person to walk on the Moon as part of the crew of Apollo 12.

Apollo 12 crew (l-r): Pete Conrad, Richard Gordon, Alan Bean

E. Donnall Thomas (March 15, 1920 — October 20, 2012)

Nobel Prize-winning physician Thomas developed bone marrow transplantation as a treatment for leukemia.

Grace Chisholm Young (March 15, 1868 — March 29, 1944)

Young was the first woman to receive a doctorate in Germany. She received the Gamble Prize for her work on calculus.

Josef Loschmidt (March 15, 1821 — July 8, 1895)

Pioneering chemist and physicist Josef Loschmidt is known for the Loschmidt Constant and Loschmidt's Paradox.

Sports

Antti Autti (March 15, 1985 —)

Finnish snowboarding star Antti-Matias Autti won the gold medal in the superpipe in the 2005 X Games, the first non-American to win the event. He also won two gold medals at the FIS Snowboarding World Championships in 2005.

Olivier Jean (March 15, 1984 —)

Olivier Jean won the gold medal in the 5000m speed skating relay in the 2010 Vancouver Olympics, and won thee gold medals in the 2011 and 2012 World Championships.

Kevin Youkilis (March 15, 1979 —)

New York Yankee Kevin Youkilis (below) was nicknamed "Euclis: The Greek God of Walks" in the best-selling *Moneyball: The Art of Winning an Unfair Game.* He achieved a record for most consecutive errorless games at first base, and won the 2008 Hank Aaron Award.

Derek Parra (March 15, 1970 —)

Parra won a gold and silver medal in speed skating at the 2002 Salt Lake City Olympics.

Harold Baines (March 15, 1952 —)

White Sox player and coach Harold Baines has the most RBI (1,628) of any player eligible for the Hall of Fame not presently included.

Clay Matthews, Jr. (March 15, 1956 —)

Former Cleveland Browns and Atlanta Falcons linebacker Clay Matthews, Jr., is the oldest player to record a sack at 40 years, 282 days.

Bobby Bonds (March 15, 1946 — August 23, 2003)

Right fielder Bobby Bonds is the father of Barry Bonds. He was the first player to have more than two seasons of 30 home runs and 30 stolen bases, a record matched only by his son.

Iron Sheik (March 15, 1943 —)

Hossein Khosrow Ali Vaziri (حسین خسرو علی وزیری), known as the Iron Sheik, was an Iranian wrestler with the WWF and subsequently gained popularity from his appearances on *The Howard Stern Show*.

Norm Van Brocklin (March 15, 1926 — May 2, 1983)

Quarterback with the Rams and the Eagles, Van Brocklin, "The Dutchman," was inducted into the Pro Football Hall of Fame in 1971.

Punch Imlach (March 15, 1918 — December 1, 1987)

Coach Imlach is in the Hockey Hall of Fame.

Henry Saint Cyr (March 15, 1902 — July 27, 1979)

Swedish equestrian Henry Saint Cyr won four Olympic gold medals in 1952 and 1956.

Jackson Schotz (March 15, 1897 — October 26, 1986)

Track and field athlete Schotz won two gold medals in the 1920 and 1924 Olympic Games. He was beaten in the 1924 Olympics, earning a silver medal, in a race later depicted in the movie *Chariots of Fire*.

James Lightbody (March 15, 1882 — March 2, 1953)

American middle distance runner James Lightbody won six Olympic gold medals and set a world record in the 1500 metre run.

Writing

Heather Graham (March 15, 1953 —)

Under her own name and the pen name Shannon Drake, Heather Graham has written over 150 novels and novellas.

Margot Howard (March 15, 1940 —)

Original "Dear Prudence" Margot Howard was the only child of advice columnist Eppie Lederer, better known as Ann Landers.

Madelyn Pugh (March 15, 1921 — April 20, 2011)

Variously credited as Madelyn Pugh Davis, Madelyn Davis, and Madelyn Martin, television writer Pugh was known for her work on *I Love Lucy, The Mothers-In-Law,* and *Alice.*

Lawrence Sanders (March 15, 1920 — February 7, 1998)

Novelist Lawrence Sanders is known for *The Anderson Tapes* and many other mystery and suspense novels. He received an Edgar Award for Best Novel in 1971.

Who Died on March 15?

Acting and Film

Ron Silver (July 2, 1946 — March 15, 2009)

Silver appeared in the sitcom *Rhoda*, appeared in the movies *Enemies: A Love Story, Reversal of Fortune, Timecop,* and *American Tragedy,* and had a recurring role in the TV series *The West Wing*. He hosted a radio show on politics and public affairs and performed various public roles for the George W. Bush administration.

Stuart Rosenberg (August 11, 1927 — March 15, 2007)

Rosenberg directed *Cool Hand Luke, Voyage of the Damned,* and *The Amityville Horror.*

Dame Thora Hird (May 28, 1911 — March 15, 2003)

Thora Hird (right) won two BAFTA Best Actress Awards and appeared in numerous British films and television series.

Ann Sothern (January 22, 1909 — March 15, 2001)

Ann Sothern appeared as *Maisie* in the comedy series of the same name, and was the lead in TV's *Private Secretary* and *The Ann Sothern Show.*

Ann Sothern in *Cry Havoc*

Gail Davis (October 5, 1925 — March 15, 1997)

Davis starred as the title character in the 1950s TV Western *Annie Oakley.*

Miles Malleson (May 25, 1888 — March 15, 1969)

British actor Malleson is known as the Sultan in 1940's *Thief of Baghdad* (which he co-wrote), the hangman in 1949's *Kind Hearts and Coronets*, and as Dr. Chasuble in 1952's *The Importance of Being Earnest.* Late in life he appeared in various Hammer horror films.

Art

Salvator Rosa (1615— March 15, 1673)

Italian Baroque painter Rosa is known as a proto-Romantic. His landscapes in particular influenced later artists in the Romantic tradition.

Self-portrait of Salvator Rosa

Business

Aristotle Onassis (Αριστοτέλης Ωνάσης) (January 15, 1906 — March 15, 1975)

Shipping magnate Aristotle Onassis is best known as the second husband of former First Lady Jacqueline Bouvier Kennedy Onassis.

Crime and Espionage

Charles Harrelson (July 23, 1938 — March 15, 2007)

Organized crime figure Charles Harrison was convicted of assassinating Federal Judge John H. ("Maximum John") Wood, and claimed to have been involved in the assassination of John F. Kennedy. He was the father of actor Woody Harrelson.

Dmitri Polyakov (Дмитрий Поляков) (July 6, 1921 — March 15, 1988)

Soviet Major General Dmitri Polyakov was a Cold War spy for the United States, known by the CIA codenames BOURBON and ROAM and by the FBI codename TOPHAT. He was betrayed by American double agents Robert Hanssen of the FBI and Aldrich Ames of the CIA, arrested by the Soviets, and executed for treason.

Government and Politics

Nikolai Bukharin (Никола́й Ива́нович Буха́рин) (October 9 [O.S. September 27], 1888 — March 15, 1938)

Bolshevik revolutionary Bukharin was an early member of the Politburo, chaired the Communist International, and edited the newspaper *Pravda*. He was purged by Joseph Stalin in the 1930s.

Cao Cao (曹操) (155 — March 15, 220)

Posthumously known as Emperor Wu of Wei, the Han Dynasty figure of Cao Cao looms large in Chinese history. Portrayed both as a cruel and merciless tyrant and as a brilliant ruler and military genius, his poetry continues to be read in modern China. The equivalent to the English expression "Speak of the Devil…" in Chinese is "Speak of Cao Cao and Cao Cao arrives." (說曹操，曹操到)

Music

Lester Young (August 27, 1909 — March 15, 1959)

Jazz tenor sax and clarinet player Lester Young (below), nicknamed "Prez," began with Count Basie and went on to develop most of the hipster ethos that accompanied cool jazz.

Science and Engineering

Sir William Pickering (December 24, 1910 — March 15, 2004)

New Zealand-born Pickering led NASA's Jet Propulsion Laboratory (JPL) for 22 years.

Benjamin Spock (May 2, 1903 — March 15, 1998)

Dr. Spock wrote the best-selling *Baby and Child Care* and helped shape a generation. In college, he won an Olympic gold medal in rowing.

Arthur Compton (September 10, 1892 — March 15, 1962)

Nobel-winning physicist Arthur Compton was an early member of the Manhattan Project. He is known for such concepts as the Compton effect, Compton length, Compton scattering, and the Compton shift. Compton Crater on the Moon is named for him.

Henry Bessemer (January 19, 1813 — March 15, 1898)

English engineer Henry Bessemer is best known for his Bessemer process for steel manufacturing.

Sports

Ken Reardon (April 1, 1921 — March 15, 2008)

Defenceman Kenny Reardon played for the NHL Montreal Canadiens and was inducted into the Hockey Hall of Fame in 1966.

Bowie Kuhn (October 28, 1926 — March 15, 2007)

Kuhn was the fifth person to serve as Commissioner of Major League Baseball.

Tom Harmon (September 28, 1919 — March 15, 1990)

Tom Harmon won the 1940 Heisman Trophy with the Michigan Wolverines and was elected to the College Football Hall of Fame. He won a Silver Star as an Army Air Corps pilot in World War II and subsequently worked as a sports broadcaster. He is the father of actor Mark Harmon and grandfather of actress Tracy Nelson and twins Matthew and Gunnar Nelson, the latter two performing as the rock group Nelson.

Abe Saperstein (July 4, 1902 — March 15, 1966)

Saperstein was commissioner of the American Basketball League and named the Harlem Globetrotters. He is the shortest member of the Basketball Hall of Fame.

Writing

Rebecca West (December 21, 1892 — March 15, 1983)

One of the most prominent public intellectuals of the 20th century, West covered the Nuremberg trial for *The New Yorker*. In 1947, *Time* Magazine said that she was "indisputably the world's number one woman writer." She was knighted in 1959.

H. P. Lovecraft (August 20, 1890 — March 15, 1937)

American fantasy and horror writer H. P. Lovecraft pioneered the "weird fiction" subgenre with his Cthulhu Mythos stories. Although not popular in his time, he has become known, in Stephen King's words, "the twentieth century's greatest practitioner of the classic horror tale.

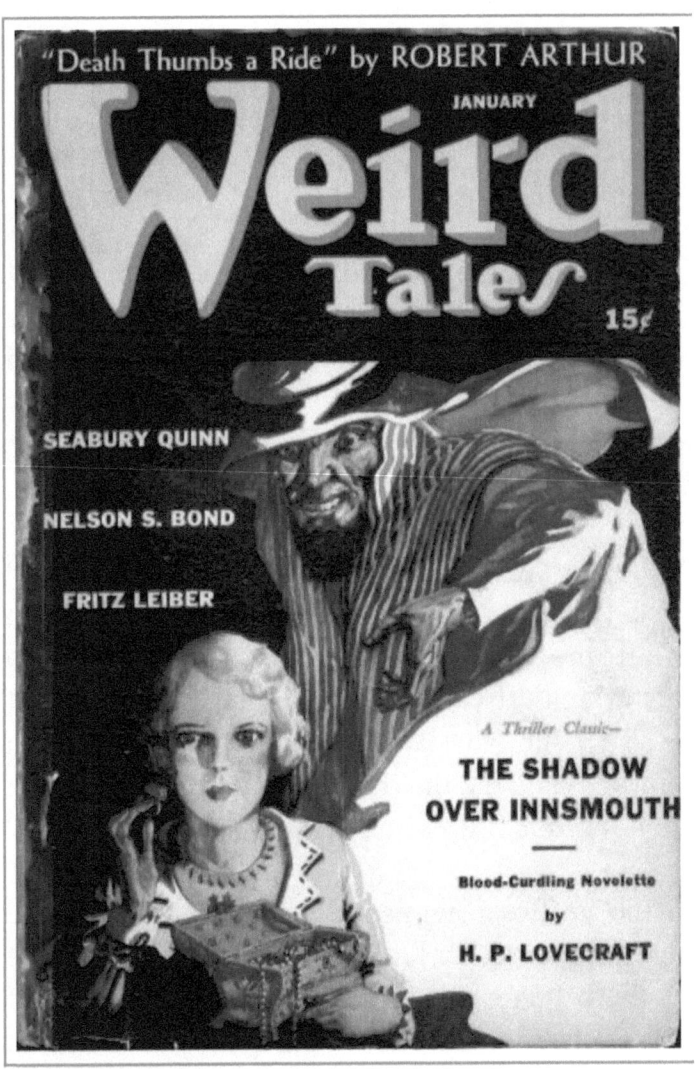

Weird Tales, January 1942, featuring a Lovecraft story

March: The Third Month

In ancient Rome, March was the first month of the year. As the first month of spring, in the Mediterranean climate it marked the beginning of the military campaign season. That's why March (Martius) is named in honor of Mars, the Roman god of war.

Although the first month of the year was moved back to January sometime during the transition of Rome from a kingdom to a republic (historians differ), March was the first month of the year in Russia until the end of the 15th Century, and is the first month of the year in many other cultures and religions.

In the northern hemisphere, March 1 marks the beginning of meteorological spring. In the southern hemisphere, March is the equivalent of September, making southern hemisphere March the beginning of autumn.

March is one of the seven months that have 31 days in it. March starts on the same day of the week as November every year, and except for leap years starts on the same day as February. March starts on the same day of the week as the previous June except for leap years, and in leap years starts on the same day as the previous September and December.

March in Other Cultures

In Finland, March is called *maaliskuu* (earthy month). In Ukraine, it's *березень* (birch tree). Other names for March include *Lentmonat* (Saxon), *Hyld-monath* (Angles), and *sušec* (Slovene).

March Symbols

Birthstones: Aquamarine and bloodstone, both representing courage.

Aquamarine

Birth Flowers: Daffodils

Daffodils in Bagatelle Park, Paris, France

March Events

Honorary months: Presidents, Congresses, and nations around the world issue proclamations recognizing particular months to honor certain causes. These events generally fall in March. (All US unless otherwise noted.)

- National Nutrition Month

- American Red Cross Month

- Women's History Month (celebrated in Canada during October)

- Irish-American Heritage Month

- Colorectal Cancer Awareness Month

- Fire Prevention Month (The Philippines)

"March Madness": (United States) The NCAA Men's Division I Basketball Championship, popularly known as "March Madness" or the "Big Dance," is a single-elimination tournament to establish the champion college basketball team.

Multi-day events: Some March events span multiple days.

- **Nineteen Day Fast:** (Bahá'í Faith) March 2 through March 20

- **Girl Scout Week:** (U.S.) The week that includes March 12, the date of the founding of the first chapter of the Girl Scouts of the USA in 1912. The earliest Girl Scout Week can start is March 6, and the latest it can end is March 18. The Sunday of Girl Scout Week is celebrated by some churches as Girl Scout Sunday or Girl Scout Sabbath.

- **Multiple Sclerosis Awareness Week:** (U.S.) Sponsored by the National Multiple Sclerosis Society, MS Awareness Week is normally held on the second full week in March. The earliest it can begin is March 9 and the latest it can end is March 21

Movable events: Some events change dates from year to year.

- **Passion Sunday:** The fifth Sunday of the Christian season of Lent is known as Passion Sunday in various Protestant denominations and by some traditionalist Catholics. Sometimes, the sixth Sunday of Lent is referred to as Passion Sunday, but it is more commonly known as Palm Sunday. Passion Sunday starts the two week Passiontide, which ends on Holy Saturday, the day before Easter, commemorating the day that Jesus's body was laid in the tomb. The fifth Sunday of Lent can occur as early as March 8 (though the next time it will be that early is in 2285 CE), and as late as April 11.

- **Palm Sunday:** The moveable feast of Palm Sunday commemorates the triumphant entry of Jesus into Jerusalem, an event mentioned in all four gospels. In many Christian churches, palm leaves are distributed to the worshippers. The earliest date for Palm Sunday is March 15, and the latest is April 18.

The month of March, from the illuminated manuscript *Les Très Riches Heures du duc de Berry*

March Zodiac Signs

From the perspective of someone on Earth, the Sun appears to move through the sky throughout the year, along a path astronomers call the ecliptic plane. The ecliptic plane is divided into twelve constellations, known as the zodiac, based on traditionally observed patterns of stars. On your birthday, you can't see your constellation, because it's part of the daytime sky.

The zodiac was first developed by Babylonian astronomers about 2,500 years ago. Because they were unaware that the Earth wobbles like a spinning top (a motion known as *precession*), they didn't make allowance for the fact that the Sun's path through the zodiac changes over time. That means there are now two sets of dates for your birth sign. The tropical dates are the original Babylonian dates; the siderial dates tell you where the Sun actually appears as it moves along its annual path.

March 15 is one of the few days that has the same astrological sign in both systems: Pisces.

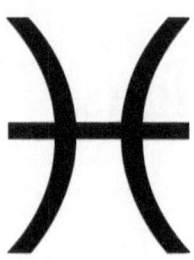

Pisces

Tropical February 20 to March 20

Siderial March 15 to April 14

In the Roman legend of Venus and her son Cupid, they escaped the clutches of Typhon, known as the "father of all monsters," by transforming into fish and tying themselves together with rope. That's why the name Pisces is plural for fish. The constellation appears as a somewhat ragged "V" shape, representing the rope, with the "fish" located at the two rope ends.

In astrology, Pisces is a water sign, compatible with the other water signs Cancer and Scorpio, as well as with the earth signs Taurus, Virgo, and Capricorn. Pisceans are supposed to be imaginative, compassionate, unworldly, secretive, and escapist.

What Day of the Week is March 15?

On what day of the week does March 15 fall?

Surprisingly, this isn't an easy question. Because the calendar year is 365 days long (366 in leap years), it doesn't divide evenly by the seven days of the week.

Also, the Earth goes around the Sun in about 365-1/4 days, so a calendar tends to drift over time. That's why the same date falls on different weekdays in different years.

This is made even more complicated by a change in calendars that took place in 1582. Our modern calendar has its roots in ancient Rome, in a calendar reform conducted by Julius Caesar. Caesar commissioned mathematicians to attack the problem, and came up with the idea of *leap years,* and thus standardized the calendar for centuries to come. This was called the *Julian calendar.*

Over time, however, the small errors in Caesar's calculation compounded. That's why Pope Gregory XIII commissioned the *Gregorian calendar,* used in most of the world today. Some countries converted in 1582, when the calendar was first developed; some converted later; other still haven't changed.

Gregorian and Julian aren't the only types of calendars. The Hebrew year, the Islamic year, and many other calendars are used in different parts of the world and among different people.

You can convert Gregorian dates to other calendars, including the Hebrew calendar, the Islamic calendar, and even the Mayan calendar by visiting the Fourmilab Calendar Converter at http://www.fourmilab.ch/documents/calendar/.

A 50-year brass perpetual calendar.

Copyright, Credit, and Contact

Follow Us

Our blog Dobson's Improbable History features short articles on events and people associated with each day, and updates several times each week. Get the latest on Twitter @SidewiseThinker.

Sources and Art Credits

All art and photographs are either in the public domain or used under a Creative Commons license. Attribution is provided where requested by the copyright owner or when of historical significance, listed below.

- The marble bust of Julius Caesar is located in the Museo Archeologico Nazionale di Napoli. The photograph was taken by Andreas Wahra, who has released it into the public domain.

- The painting *Rise Up, Hungarian!* is by János Thorma, and is in the public domain because its copyright has expired.

- The 1670s portrait of Charles II of England is by Peter Lely and is in the public domain because its copyright has expired.

- The painting of revolutionary troops at the Battle of Guilford Court House was an original work commissioned by the U.S. government, and is in the public domain.

- The 1905 Rolls-Royce 10HP in the Manchester Museum of Science and Industry was photographed by an unknown photographer, and is used under the Creative Commons Attribution-Share Alike 2.0 UK: England & Wales license.

- The 1913 portrait photograph of Tsar Nicholas II and his family is in the collection of the Hermitage Museum in St. Petersburg. It is in the public domain because its copyright has expired.

- The 2011 photograph of Joaquim de Almeida was taken by Ricardo Silva and is used here under the Creative Commons Attribution 3.0 Unported license.

- The publicity photograph of Joe E. Ross and Fred Gwynne from *Car 54, Where Are You?* is in the public domain because it was published between 1923 and 1977 without a copyright notice.

- The photograph of Fergie and will.i.am at the 2011 Walmart Shareholder's Meeting was provided by Walmart and is used under the Creative Commons Attribution 2.0 Generic license.

- The portrait of Lightnin' Hopkins is by Jules Grandgagnage, and is used here under the Creative Commons Attribution-Share Alike 3.0 Unported license.

- The official Supreme Court portrait of Ruth Bader Ginsburg is in the public domain as a work of the U.S. federal government.

- The portrait of Andrew Jackson is by Thomas Sully. It is in the public domain because its copyright has expired.

- The photograph of the crew of Apollo 12 is in the public domain as a work of NASA.

- The 2009 photograph of Kevin Youkilis was taken by Keith Allison and is used here under the Creative Commons Attribution-Share Alike 2.0 Generic license.

- The 1973 photograph of Dame Thora Hird was taken by Allan Warren and is used here under the Creative Commons Attribution-Share Alike 3.0 Unported license.

- The screenshot of Ann Sothern from the *Cry Havoc* trailer is in the public domain because it was published between 1923 and 1977 without a copyright notice.

- The 1946 photograph of Lester Young at the Famous Door in New York was taken by William P. Gottlieb and is taken from the William P. Gottlieb Collection at the Library of Congress Music Division. At the wishes of the donor, the photographs in this collection are in the public domain.

Timespinner
Press